The
YOU
After...
WE

Tellwell Talent

www.tellwell.ca

ISBN

978-1-77370-048-9 (Paperback)

The YOU After...WE

A sacred "*scribery*" for the sassy and single.

Here is your break-up journal – a grieving guidance counsellor for the loss of your relationship. However the split went down, however long ago, it will leave a mark. But watch those scars fade over time, and let this be a tool for your journey with some insight for your mind, and a few jabs for your funny bone.

Use your emotions to format your journal, and be inspired by some of my personal experiences, a few conventional insights, and yes, cynical blurbs too. This is where you write, jot, and draw your way to a redefined you.

As you transform your life from the WE that is no longer, guess who will be left standing? YOU.

The new, stronger, better than ever YOU!

This journal belongs to:

_____

A WE as at:

_____

YOU:

FOREVER MORE

From ME to YOU

Here's the thing. I'm a numbers gal and a wee bit social media adverse too. So why am I sharing words and personal stories with you? Why should you use or share this journal, read my quips, use it as a resource for self expression, or as a tool to help find "YOU" again?

Because above all, I am empathetic, I am passionate, and whole heartedly believe in THE POWER OF PERSPECTIVE.

I feel compelled to convey personal insights from my "been there, done that" experiences. I feel compelled to help and apply the theory of strength in numbers; you are not alone. Okay, so I tend to be wordy and generally live for a laugh, and this was an ideal platform for that too!

Frankly it can just suck when you are thrown a life lemon (pardon the pun); or you are in the thick of a major life transition – bad or even good. During these times of change you may feel a loss, whether it's literally part of your life, or parts of your identity. In dealing with that loss, I feel some women may find it difficult to process their thoughts and emotions without judgment, or finding that other "G" spot... yeah, the guilt complex.

During major life transitions of my own, I realized the constructive power of support and validation from others, in all its various forms. Generally, I think we not only crave this backing (secretly or not), but can use it to endure the not-so-certain times of life. I am also a big believer of expression through words, and yes, often way too many of them!

So I became passionate about combining those concepts. I wanted to promote the simple keys of comfort that I used while navigating my bumps in the road; to read, write, and, above all, laugh. I wanted to create a support tool for others, an outlet to rationalize, scream, cry, and revel about life.

My story leading up to this point is a classic tale. Upon graduating university and getting a job, I married my school sweetheart. My career took off and I was climbing a quick ladder to success. But after our first child was born I slowed things down and opted to work part-time, to ensure I could be a fully engaged Mom too; the most prominent, challenging and wonderful role of my life.

My husband's company and career blossomed, we had another child, and I was balancing work and home life with two kids the best I could. We spent years renovating our entire home in a great neighbourhood. We escaped the city and enjoyed his family cottage, travelled, and were part of a huge family and friend network. Life was good, typical, planned, and from anyone who knew us, we were "that" couple.

Then one day it happened. My marriage came to an end. When my world blew up, so to speak, marriage breakdown, followed by my corporate division closing down, I decided the world was trying to tell me something. I took the time to revisit who I was, and, more importantly, who I wanted to be.

I am into the groove of my new normal. From explaining the unexplainable to my kids, to taking on life as a single gal, I can relate to the loss of being a "WE" for more than half my life. The roller coaster and path I took to get here today was not easy. My friends and family, an unscathed sense of humour, and the power of perspective guided me on that ride; in fact, all of it has made me a better person in the end. That should be the goal of any life transition, *a better YOU... after.*

Now I find myself here on a new journey, to provide support and smiles to those who find themselves in a funk; specifically, women dealing with major life changes I can relate to. I want to hug every single one of them, crack an inappropriate joke, to crack an oh so necessary smile. But to do this one person at a time is not convenient as a single mom!

I have heard the words "you should write a book or share your thoughts" more than once in my life.

So this is me, just wanting to spread some optimism wrapped in cynicism to you.

This is your hug.

The YOU After... WE

"The You After..." journal
by Sally Donovan

So here you are, "uncoupled".

Consciously or not, uncoupling from a WE means a transformation of YOU. It is a change, and regardless of circumstance, there will be some sort of mental and emotional toll to pay.

Lose the tether and get your "uncoupled" self journaling to help sort through your mind space; the rational and well, the not so much.

The pages ahead in your sacred "scribery" are set up to help you deal with the emotional roller coaster of the loss of your relationship. You will see many sides to yourself, at different times, and in no particular direction. That's right, emotions are not logical (sigh, that hurts the left side of my brain). How and when to scribe your thoughts, well, that is up to you.

The main moments you will find yourself in will be Denial & Hope, Anger, Sadness and Acceptance. So let me introduce you to them, my good pals that you will meet along your journey to redefining YOU.

DENIAL & HOPE: Feign Friends.

Think air kisses and "Hello Darling".
They seem so perfect on the outside, but you know underneath all that fluff, there is zero substance.

ANGER: Leather Clad Diva.

Nuff said.
She is there when you don't give a sh#$ about what anyone else thinks.
This is no holds barred territory.

SADNESS: Frumpy Flannel Fran.

She hides under the covers never to be seen; until you run out of ice cream of course.

She is there when you don't give a sh#$ about anything...and you will have those days.

ACCEPTANCE: The YOU After WE.

She is in you, just wait and see.

Gorgeous, peaceful, changed and better than ever.

Hello YOU!

There you go. Your new posse.

So whatever MOMENT you are in, take pen to paper to get out your thoughts and clear your mind. Scribe away to help sort through the new YOU.

But above all else, hang on to your sense of humour.
IT WILL SAVE YOUR SOUL!

What Moment Are YOU In?

In the Moment of...

Denial & Hope

Umm, WTF?

This can <u>not</u> be happening.

Then one day it happened.

After our typical summer of cottage time, family gatherings and even a couples trip to California had ended, he told me. My husband had fallen out of love with me.

So was this a big shock? Well if I look back, he had distanced himself in the months leading up to his declaration. That said, our relationship of almost 20 years had its ups and downs and he wasn't communicator of the year, by his own admission. Another blip I thought. When I felt that he was building a wall, I thought we would get through it like we always had. I did not expect that this wall was being engineered without an exit door.

My first reaction was simply denial.

Alright, I've got this. Solution mode meets hope. Most companies would have revelled in the determination and rationality of my approach. I was going to fix this. We need to work on our relationship, I hear you. It was always kids first, work first, oh and let's not forget to mention multiple home renovations. If life wasn't stressful enough, we took on major annual home improvement projects, and lived in the house through each one. A roof over your head is highly overrated, when a blue tarp can do the job for a while!

So obviously I thought my husband's issue about love was correlated with lack of attention. I agreed things needed to change- counselling, a trip, date nights, I would ease up on my pent up resentment, and yes, I was going to try using a filter before I speak (I come by this trait honestly). This was a great wake up call to turn our priorities around. Actually, despite the big pit in my stomach, I thought this may be good for me, for us. A fresh start on our relationship, how exciting!

But deep down it did not feel right. The hope was masking my logic. Deep down I was scared. What if I couldn't fix this? But more so, what if he didn't want to fix it?

I had led a successful life thus far. So really, failing at my marriage and ultimately my family, was not an option here. There had to be a solution.

But here's the thing that I didn't let myself absorb at that point. Marriage is consensual between two people. It has to be. Separation on the other hand, does not need to be. It takes just one person to break up the union. Now isn't that an effing kick in the pants!

Here lay the pages to express the confusion you may have over your relationship breakdown. Write out your questions, thoughts and hopes. Hope for any aspect of the grieving – to rekindle, for forgiveness, to find happiness. Even if your thoughts seem irrational or unfounded, hope has its place in healing. For some, it can dull the pain just enough to carry on with life, until they find themselves in a different "moment". For others it may seem like a waste of time and a prolonging phase, as they just want to move on.

Kind of like pregnant women in labour who either want an epidural as soon as they enter the hospital, or conversely choose natural childbirth... even 18 hours in. Different process, but both ladies end up "pushing" through to the end.

_____

_____

_____

_____

_____

_____

_____

_____

_____

_____

_____

_____

_____

_____

_____

_____

_____

_____

_____

_____

_____

_____

_____

_____

_____

_____

_____

_____

_____

_____

_____

_____

_____

_____

_____

_____

_____

_____

_____

_____

_____

The YOU After...WE

_____

_____

_____

_____

_____

_____

_____

_____

_____

_____

_____

_____

_____

_____

_____

_____

_____

_____

_____

When you think "I" can fix "us", remember you are up against one heck of an oxymoron.

_____

_____

_____

_____

_____

_____

_____

_____

_____

_____

_____

_____

_____

_____

_____

_____

_____

_____

_____

_____

Hope takes justification to a whole new professional level. You will master the skill of dissecting spoken and written words, until you piece together what you WANT to hear.

If only you could add "Post-Relationship Forensic Scientist" to your resume.

_____

_____

_____

_____

_____

_____

_____

_____

_____

_____

_____

_____

_____

_____

_____

_____

_____

_____

_____

_____

_____

Listen _____

(ex's name here)

I'm not always right, I am just very good at laying out the truth!

_____

_____

_____

_____

_____

_____

_____

_____

_____

_____

_____

_____

_____

_____

_____

_____

_____

_____

_____

_____

_____

_____

*It takes **two** people to build a relationship,*

*yet just **one** person to tear it down.*

Where are the laws of physics when you need them most?

_____

_____

_____

_____

_____

_____

_____

_____

_____

_____

_____

_____

_____

_____

_____

_____

_____

_____

_____

_____

When you think this is just a "time out", remember relationships don't have game clocks.

_____

_____

_____

_____

_____

_____

_____

_____

_____

_____

_____

_____

_____

_____

_____

_____

_____

_____

_____

_____

Stop e-pestering.

Put your hands up and step away from the phone!

_____

_____

_____

_____

_____

_____

_____

_____

_____

_____

_____

_____

_____

_____

_____

_____

_____

_____

_____

_____

_____

It is one thing to fight to get your ex to walk back on your door mat.

It's another to be the door mat in doing so.

_____

_____

_____

_____

_____

_____

_____

_____

_____

_____

_____

_____

_____

_____

_____

_____

_____

_____

Hope fights logic.

Cut yourself some slack because damn,
hope can throw one hell of a punch!

_____

_____

_____

_____

_____

_____

_____

_____

_____

_____

_____

_____

_____

_____

_____

_____

_____

_____

_____

They should have warning pop ups on messaging apps like they do on cigarette packages.

WARNING: E-stalking can cause regret and heartache.

_____

_____

_____

_____

_____

_____

_____

_____

_____

_____

_____

_____

_____

_____

_____

_____

_____

_____

_____

_____

_____

_____

No response can be louder than words
and harder to hear.

_____

_____

_____

_____

_____

_____

_____

_____

_____

_____

_____

_____

_____

_____

_____

_____

_____

_____

_____

_____

_____

_____

_____

_____

_____

_____

_____

_____

_____

_____

_____

_____

_____

_____

_____

_____

_____

_____

_____

_____

_____

_____

_____

_____

_____

_____

_____

_____

_____

_____

_____

_____

_____

_____

_____

_____

_____

_____

_____

_____

_____

_____

_____

_____

_____

_____

_____

_____

_____

_____

_____

_____

_____

_____

_____

_____

_____

_____

_____

_____

_____

_____

_____

_____

_____

_____

_____

_____

_____

_____

_____

_____

_____

_____

_____

_____

_____

_____

_____

_____

_____

_____

_____

_____

_____

_____

_____

_____

_____

_____

_____

_____

_____

_____

_____

_____

_____

_____

_____

_____

_____

_____

_____

_____

_____

_____

_____

_____

_____

_____

_____

_____

_____

_____

_____

_____

_____

_____

_____

_____

_____

_____

_____

_____

_____

_____

_____

_____

_____

_____

_____

_____

_____

_____

_____

_____

_____

_____

_____

_____

_____

_____

_____

_____

_____

_____

_____

_____

_____

_____

_____

_____

_____

_____

_____

_____

_____

_____

_____

_____

_____

_____

_____

_____

_____

_____

_____

_____

_____

_____

_____

_____

_____

_____

_____

_____

_____

_____

_____

_____

_____

_____

_____

_____

_____

_____

_____

_____

_____

_____

_____

_____

_____

_____

_____

_____

_____

_____

_____

_____

_____

_____

_____

_____

_____

_____

_____

_____

_____

_____

_____

_____

_____

_____

_____

_____

_____

_____

_____

_____

_____

_____

_____

_____

_____

_____

_____

_____

_____

_____

_____

_____

_____

_____

_____

_____

_____

_____

_____

_____

_____

_____

_____

_____

_____

_____

_____

_____

_____

_____

_____

_____

_____

In the Moment of...

Anger

The Prickly Pages.

As in, if I had a voodoo doll of my ex, the first prick
of the pin would go here...prick, prick, prick!

I love you, but I'm not *in* love with you.

Ironically, he had it all wrong. Looking back at that moment I now know it was backwards. I'm *in* love with you but I don't love you as much as (fill in blank here): my job, a new her, my freedom, or all of the above.

I'm still *in* love with the idea of you...my partner, wife, mother of my children, family CEO, financial adviser, income generator, social butterfly, and still not too bad on the eyes woman.... I'm *in* love with what you are on paper. Yeah, but I don't love the responsibilities, compromises and communication most of that entails. I don't love dealing with life's ups and downs, or handling the natural resentments and hard work of a relationship anymore.

Lies, stress, guilt, revoked responsibilities...eventually anger reared its ugly head despite the longing for hope. My tongue should have bled from biting it so hard, as I held back the vile things I wanted to say. And well, sometimes they were said, which did not prove productive.

But anger led me to a new relationship with rationality, and understanding how the most important thing you can control is what you say. When enraged, I found myself writing more (yes, a few pencils were harmed during this time). It allowed me to express in a more benign way – I had the freedom I needed to blow up, but ensuring no casualties would be had from the explosion.

As kryptonite is to Superman, rationality is to anger.

Anger also led me to a new relationship with boxing gloves. I joined a kick-boxing gym shortly after my marriage started to break down. For me the physical outlet was like no other. My mental therapy was kicking and punching the emotions that came with all of this. I left it all on the floor, in the ring, in a pile of sweat, and picked myself up again for the real battle with my new reality.

Here lay the pages to help calm you down when you are, well, effing pissed off by the whole situation. So write, draw pictures, or stab randomly at the pages. Think of this as the cooling off zone before you share your thoughts, words or (let's hope not) stabs with anyone else! This is also a great place to keep a list of rebuttals that will organically come up, as you write in a heated state of mind.

This section is rated R for coarse language.

_____

_____

_____

_____

_____

_____

_____

_____

_____

_____

_____

_____

_____

_____

_____

_____

_____

_____

_____

_____

_____

_____

_____

_____

_____

_____

_____

_____

_____

_____

_____

_____

_____

_____

_____

_____

_____

_____

_____

_____

_____

_____

May you always remember that when life hands you lemons,
you need to learn how to throw really, really hard.

Now having a target is merely a bonus.

_____

_____

_____

_____

_____

_____

_____

_____

_____

_____

_____

_____

_____

_____

_____

_____

_____

_____

_____

_____

Women bear children and wear heels.

The dude who first uttered the words
"life is not fair",
takes stating the obvious to the next level.

After the fairy Princess marries her Prince,
only 50% of the fairy tales should read
"THEY LIVED HAPPILY EVER AFTER".

The other 50% should just skip right to
"THE END".

The YOU After...WE

_____

_____

_____

_____

_____

_____

_____

_____

_____

_____

_____

_____

_____

_____

_____

_____

_____

_____

_____

_____

_____

Marriage certificates should have best before dates on them.

If you pass that milestone, then that is the Golden Anniversary!

Do you, John, take thee Jane to be your wedded wife?

"I do...until I don't want to".

There is something to be said about honesty.

_____

_____

_____

_____

_____

_____

_____

_____

_____

_____

_____

_____

_____

_____

_____

_____

_____

_____

_____

_____

_____

And there will be days when you want to wear a t-shirt that says:

I call Bull Sh#$!
It would have been better to have never loved you at all.

_____

_____

_____

_____

_____

_____

_____

_____

_____

_____

_____

_____

_____

_____

_____

_____

_____

_____

_____

_____

_____

_____

And then one day you traded in
the ice cream quart for boxing gloves.

Punching therapy is a thing.

_____

_____

_____

_____

_____

_____

_____

_____

_____

_____

_____

_____

_____

_____

_____

_____

_____

_____

_____

_____

_____

_____

_____

_____

Go on, be a Princess.

You can throw one hell of a hard kick in glass slippers!

_____

_____

_____

_____

_____

_____

_____

_____

_____

_____

_____

_____

_____

_____

_____

_____

_____

_____

_____

_____

_____

_____

If "Video Killed the Radio Star",
then Cynicism Killed the Romance Star.

_____

_____

_____

_____

_____

_____

_____

_____

_____

_____

_____

_____

_____

_____

_____

_____

_____

_____

_____

_____

_____

_____

_____

_____

_____

_____

_____

_____

_____

_____

_____

_____

_____

_____

_____

_____

_____

_____

_____

_____

_____

_____

_____

_____

_____

_____

_____

_____

_____

_____

_____

_____

_____

_____

_____

_____

_____

_____

_____

_____

_____

_____

_____

_____

_____

_____

_____

_____

_____

_____

_____

_____

_____

_____

_____

_____

_____

_____

_____

_____

_____

_____

_____

_____

_____

_____

_____

_____

_____

_____

_____

_____

_____

_____

_____

_____

_____

_____

_____

_____

_____

_____

_____

_____

_____

_____

_____

_____

_____

_____

_____

_____

_____

_____

_____

_____

_____

_____

_____

_____

_____

_____

_____

_____

_____

_____

_____

_____

_____

_____

_____

_____

_____

_____

_____

_____

_____

_____

_____

_____

_____

_____

_____

_____

_____

_____

_____

_____

_____

_____

_____

_____

_____

_____

_____

_____

_____

_____

_____

_____

_____

_____

_____

_____

_____

_____

_____

_____

_____

In the Moment of...

Sadness

A whole lot of tissues.

A wee bit of Adele.

The months that followed were like none other.

I was at a loss, but the show must go on. Work, birthday parties, family functions. In my situation I still wasn't sure what was happening, and did not want to talk to anyone about it. I was living in a fog of sadness.

But my body was not having any of it. I could not sleep through the night, I lost my appetite, and had a pit in my stomach at all times. I was on a new diet unbeknownst to me!

Sadness was eating away at me. It was physically changing me. Obviously I knew that stress could affect your whole body, but didn't understand it. I guess I thought you could fight the symptoms by not giving in to what you can control....but how do you control the untameable?

Like most people, I did not give Mental Stress (I will capitalize it now, because it is a persona, thing of importance) the respect it deserved. I am a left brained person (or a right brained person trapped in a left minded body, am still unsure), so I guess I thought you could fix mental states with logic and rationality.

You just push through it.

You just push through it.

Oh what a fighter, right? She is so strong, right? Superhero status - means yay for my ego, but woe is me.

I had never felt worse in my life. To go back, ask for help sooner, share my story sooner, seek the attention my body and mind were begging for; I would have been better off.

Pushing through is not winning. It's just that...pushing away the inevitable. Not embracing and soaking in the now, and dealing with it head on.

Give sadness and stress its deserved time to be able to move forward. Stop, listen and change things, even temporarily to deal with your current state of mind.

Those who embrace mental health, those are the people who deserve the superhero cape.

Here lay the pages to express yourself when you have that whole ugly cry, can't talk thing going on. Get the yuck in your head out on paper. Document your loss, worries and fears. Articulate that pit in your stomach caused by all the things you will miss about "WE", and all the things you can't possibly face on your own....until you don't...and then do again. But until then, this is your place to unleash the sadness so it doesn't weigh you down so much. This is your safe, non-judgemental, supportive, objective space to let it all out.

Avoid markers here—the text will smear when wet.

_____

_____

_____

_____

_____

_____

_____

_____

_____

_____

_____

_____

_____

_____

_____

_____

_____

_____

_____

_____

_____

_____

_____

_____

_____

_____

_____

_____

_____

_____

_____

_____

_____

_____

_____

_____

_____

_____

_____

_____

_____

_____

_____

Let us get over the "You will get over IT" mantra shall we?!

IT is part of you now. Embrace IT, seal IT, and make sure IT doesn't leak to other parts of you.

Don't get over IT. Just don't let IT hold you back.

_____

_____

_____

_____

_____

_____

_____

_____

_____

_____

_____

_____

_____

_____

_____

_____

_____

_____

_____

_____

_____

_____

They say time heals all wounds.

Think tick tock...you are inevitably on your way.

Misery loves company. Late night with Google
will prove you are not alone.

1,240,000 pages on coping with break ups – that is comradery!

*Stress. That's Mr. Stress to you. Give stress the **RESPECT** it deserves. It will wreak havoc on your body and mind. You may need to change your ways until that Mister leaves the building.*

*Sometimes you have to screw the positive and hoity clichés
of support, and go with the grass roots words of comfort.*

"This sucks"!

While not as publicized, it is thought that wine and chocolate are to the soul, what green tea and kale are to the body.

It's all good.

_____

_____

_____

_____

_____

_____

_____

_____

_____

_____

_____

_____

_____

_____

_____

_____

_____

_____

_____

_____

_____

_____

_____

Can we dial down the LOVE fest over the holiday season please, jewellers and perfumeries?

WTF happened to world peace?

You lost your BAE, but guess what? Your BTAE is waiting for you.

BETTER THAN ANYONE ELSE !

_____
_____
_____
_____
_____
_____
_____
_____
_____
_____
_____
_____
_____
_____
_____
_____
_____
_____
_____
_____
_____

Screw Valentine's Day.

Wear black and hoard all the good chocolate now available.

You are in mourning after all.

_____

_____

_____

_____

_____

_____

_____

_____

_____

_____

_____

_____

_____

_____

_____

_____

_____

_____

_____

_____

_____

_____

_____

_____

_____

_____

_____

_____

_____

_____

_____

_____

_____

_____

_____

_____

_____

_____

_____

_____

_____

_____

_____

_____

_____

_____

_____

_____

_____

_____

_____

_____

_____

_____

_____

_____

_____

_____

_____

_____

_____

_____

_____

_____

_____

_____

_____

_____

_____

_____

_____

_____

_____

_____

_____

_____

_____

_____

_____

_____

_____

_____

_____

_____

_____

_____

_____

_____

_____

_____

_____

_____

_____

_____

_____

_____

_____

_____

_____

_____

_____

_____

_____

_____

_____

_____

_____

_____

_____

_____

_____

_____

_____

_____

_____

_____

_____

_____

_____

_____

_____

_____

_____

_____

_____

_____

_____

_____

_____

_____

_____

_____

_____

_____

_____

_____

_____

_____

_____

_____

_____

_____

_____

_____

_____

_____

_____

_____

In the Moment of...

Acceptance

You got this.

Now snap your fingers in a Z formtion!

Weeks turned to months. Despite my protests we had to tell the kids, tell our families and ultimately create a new life.

It was getting harder to hope, too tiring to be sad, and I was too apathetic to be angry.

I had absorbed, researched, read, expressed, punched, explored, and appreciated my way to healing. From denial, hope, anger and sadness, acceptance was emerging. These moments, feelings, and transformations that I dealt with head on, were parallel to a magical elixir called *time*.

It does get better with time, *only if* you embrace your posse of emotions and allow it. But it takes an undetermined, unique to you, unprecedented amount of time – uggh, I know!

You will be changed, and hopefully for the better. And life lessons will soon surface. You will learn how to be a better you, a better partner, appreciate more and ironically, that includes understanding the derailing experience you went through.

Most exciting, is that you can envision a new future of what you want for yourself and if the case, in a new partner. This was not the future you had planned, but how fantastic because it may well be a better plan. Different can be better.

For me, I knew I wanted to be somebody's Eddy...

Fast forward over a year later and in enters a new man of the house, Eddy. The cutest mini Aussiedoodle puppy that melted my heart the second I saw him. One day, I introduced Eddy to a dear practitioner friend. He had remarked how he instinctively knew I had a special bond with my pup. He said, "It is the way you hold him and look at him. He makes you smile and you know how special he is. He lights up a room and makes you feel good no matter what happened, even mere minutes ago". He then said, "You my dear, are like an Eddy". ☺

Sweet words indeed.

When I heard those words I found myself with a new quest. I was going to be somebody's Eddy! Okay, okay, not somebody's dog or pet, but be so adored and endearing to someone that there will never be a question of connection or conditions. More so, I wanted to find my own Eddy to do that for me.

Don't worry boy, you are irreplaceable. But at that moment, I regained hope in love and *accepting* of what the future could hold for me.

Ha, guess you can teach an old dog new tricks.

Here lay the pages to revel in your new found peace. Congratulations, you did it!

Whether it be a few minutes or many weeks of acceptance you can write about, you can still taste the transformation. This is the holding place for your personal positive clichés on steroids. Write about the past you are over, the good of the now, and the excitement of perhaps an even better tomorrow.

This section is best enjoyed with a fine wine and Gloria Gaynor playing in the background.

Just think, a "new" normal is on the horizon!

So make it a good one.

I am thankful for wine, sarcasm, the delete button, and all the things we shouldn't say out loud that we are REALLY thankful for (nudge, nudge, wink, wink ;)

One day I got talking to an 85 year old European woman on the subway. As she left the train, she gave me some advice to remember while I was ACCEPTING my new life...

(Read slowly in a thick "Germanesk" accent)

"You don't need to be married to have THE sex".

Well, she does raise a good point.

It's a shame for life to kick you in the ass and not learn from it.

Then it's just a useless bruise that never goes away.

Height expressed under 6 feet tall on a man's dating profile, does not translate to the correct imperial or metric unit of measure. In fact, a consistent conversion rate is still unknown at this time.

(Read: He ain't as tall as he says.)

*I fell in love with my dog in one minute and
will receive unconditional love for his lifetime.*

Beat that guarantee online dating site!

_____

_____

_____

_____

_____

_____

_____

_____

_____

_____

_____

_____

_____

_____

_____

_____

_____

_____

_____

_____

_____

_____

Ever feel too old to have a "boy" friend or "girl" friend?

But "This is Bob, my Version 2.0" does not seem apt either.

DENIAL, HOPEFUL, ANGRY or SAD moments are temporary because you will end up here.

ACCEPTING a new life, a new YOU!

Hold on to that thought.

_____

_____

_____

_____

_____

_____

_____

_____

_____

_____

_____

_____

_____

_____

_____

_____

_____

_____

_____

_____

_____

Experience is a beautiful thing.

*You rising up from this means if you are ever down again, you **KNOW** you can get back up.*

What a gift for your future!

_____

_____

_____

_____

_____

_____

_____

_____

_____

_____

_____

_____

_____

_____

_____

_____

_____

_____

_____

_____

_____

_____

_____

_____

_____

_____

_____

_____

_____

_____

_____

_____

_____

_____

_____

_____

_____

_____

_____

_____

_____

_____

_____

_____

_____

_____

_____

_____

_____

_____

_____

_____

_____

_____

_____

_____

_____

_____

_____

_____

_____

_____

_____

_____

_____

_____

_____

_____

_____

_____

_____

_____

_____

_____

_____

_____

_____

_____

_____

_____

_____

_____

_____

_____

_____

_____

_____

_____

_____

_____

_____

_____

_____

_____

_____

_____

_____

_____

_____

_____

_____

_____

_____

May your captured thoughts serve you well.
Over time you should look back at all of these "moments".

Then you will see how far you have come,
After WE to...YOU!

Hello YOU!

One FINAL Moment

During the period when I was tackling an irrational problem with a practical approach, some of my research led to the idea of creating an objective for my marriage.

I was to create a guiding principal or belief for what I wanted my relationship to be. While it did not serve me well in my then, current affairs, I hold on to it as an axiom for my future.

A vision of what I want any new partnership to be.

Even after all this time, my quest is still the same. It serves as a reminder of not just setting expectations, but the idea of *continually* working toward, with, and for them.

With hesitation in sharing a very personal reflection, I do so in hopes to inspire you; to provide an example so you can create a boundless concept to not only obtain, but to maintain forever more.

"My mission for my marriage is to create a union based on unconditional love and support. Our marriage will be an emotional and physical haven that we both desire to be a part of, and actually, can't get enough of. We will be best friends and the pillar of support during good times and especially the harder times. We will have a marriage filled with mutual pride, compassion and respect that propels us to be the best people we can be; the best in all aspects of our life, but especially as partners to each other. A place where communication comes freely, trust is a given and appreciation is demonstrated constantly through words, actions, and touch. All this with a good sense of humour and light-heartedness instilled in whatever we do. We will strive to have a marriage that is not based on love, but IS love – because not only will it be our priority, but we will covet, to create happiness for each other".

Let this be your space to create statements of your vision; a list of attributes for a thriving relationship so you never have to fill out this damn journal again!

My next WE will be....

_____

_____

_____

_____

_____

_____

_____

_____

_____

_____

_____

_____

_____

_____

_____

_____

_____

_____

_____

_____

_____

_____

_____

_____

_____

_____

_____

_____

_____

_____

_____

_____

_____

_____

_____

_____

_____

_____

_____

About the Author

ON a mission to create books to guide women through major life transitions with insight and humour, Sally founded The YOU After. This is her first journal and the inspiration for *her* new life transition; to publish what seems to be supportive and sassy wisdom, a few sketch emojis, and some blank lines?!

After her idealistic, planned, and stable life became derailed, Sally thought she needed to try something different. She decided to take the opportunity to follow her passion of sharing unsolicited thoughts to, well, anyone who will listen. That's right - it dawned on her that you can block texts, but you can't block freedom of speech in a published book.

Her inspiration to smile, laugh and gab comes naturally from her family and what she is still trying to prove, some ancestry with clown roots.

But most of all she is driven by the unconditional love for her two beautiful daughters and darling dog (not necessarily in that order ;) She happily resides in her home in Toronto, Canada, with maybe, just maybe, one more home renovation project on the horizon.

For more unsolicited words of questionable wisdom and
"dog walking" generated thoughts, please visit her website:

TheYouAfter.com